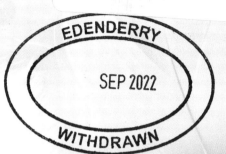

the

Year

With

Angels

Lorna Byrne has been seeing and talking to angels since she was a baby. Now that her family is raised she talks openly about what she has learned. She lives quietly in rural Ireland. She is the author of the international bestsellers *Angels in My Hair*, *Stairways to Heaven*, *A Message of Hope from the Angels* and *Love From Heaven*. Her books have been translated into over twenty languages.

LORNA BYRNE

the Year With Angels

A GUIDE TO LIVING LOVINGLY
THROUGH THE SEASONS

CORONET

First published in Great Britain in 2016 by Coronet
An imprint of Hodder & Stoughton
An Hachette UK company

1

A CIP catalogue record for this title is available from the British Library

Hardback ISBN: 978 1 473 64936 1
Ebook ISBN: 978 1 473 64935 4

Typeset in Bodini Book by www.envyltd.co.uk

Printed and bound by Lego Spa, Italy

Hodder & Stoughton policy is to use papers that are natural, renewable and
recyclable products and made from wood grown in sustainable forests. The logging
and manufacturing processes are expected to conform to the environmental
regulations of the country of origin.

Hodder & Stoughton Ltd
Carmelite House
50 Victoria Embankment
London EC4Y 0DZ

www.hodder.co.uk

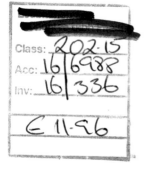

The Angel of Hope has the light of hope burning brightly in front of you. Allow your eyes to see that beacon of light, hope and love that surrounds you every moment of your life. This book is for all those who are willing to take that chance and open their eyes to the wonder around them.

Blessings, Lorna

Introduction

This book is to help you to recognise the spiritual side of yourself through the seasons of the year.

It is about awakening and feeling blessed in your life. It is about knowing that you are not alone. Your guardian angel is right there with you, the gatekeeper of your soul, loving you unconditionally.

This book is about you realising how much you are loved and cherished because inside of you is a spiritual being, your soul. Your soul, your spiritual self is a spark of light that radiates brilliantly like nothing else.

Let me help you through every season of the year so that you can become more aware of that sacred part of you. Let's walk on a journey through each season, with your guardian angel holding your hand, to help you to fill your life with more hope and laughter.

This journey will help you to enjoy being alive. Becoming aware of the spiritual side of yourself will help to open your eyes so that you see all the beauty and good things around you.

Let's start this journey together, one step at a time. Let's smile and laugh as we take each step. Even if you are nervous, know you have your guardian angel right there with you. No matter who you are or what you have done in your life your guardian angel never gives up on you, not even for one second.

Spring

Your guardian angel wants you to know what springtime can do for you.

Springtime gives us great encouragement when we see new life coming up through the earth. Trees become visibly alive, sprouting their green buds and flowers. The birds sing, letting us know that spring is here – and that our lives can start all over again. It should fill us all with hope and happiness. So wake up and allow springtime to inspire you.

It's a time of new beginnings. With another year comes another chance to change the things we want to change in our lives. A chance to strive towards a more fulfilled and joyful you.

Spring gives us the opportunity to look around, to recognize what is in our life, to decide the things that we want to hold onto and equally to decide what is in our lives that we want to let go of. Have a good look at the things you want to let go of.

Ask your guardian angel to help. Simply visualise putting what you want to let go of in a bag and then putting it in the bin. The things you want to let go of could be negative feelings of hurt, anger or jealousy, for example. Or they could even be physical changes you want to make in your life. Or it could be about moving on from heartbreak or the grief of losing a loved one.

Wake up and allow springtime to inspire you.

Every day of the year you are given the opportunity

for a new beginning.

Hope brings a community together to make things better and when it does I see people get brighter, shine more and then they can go on to achieve greater things. People who believe things can be changed for the better are beacons of light for us – and need to be supported.

No matter how lonely you may feel – you are never alone. Your guardian angel never leaves you, not for a minute; it is with you from before you are conceived and stays with you until after you are dead. It never leaves you, so no matter how alone you may feel you are never alone. It is the gatekeeper of your soul. Regardless of your religion or lack of any belief, regardless of whether you believe in angels or not, your guardian angel is there beside you waiting for you to ask for its help. You're precious to it, you're its number one. It will do everything it can for you. All you have to do is ask.

Lorna Byrne

The angels teach us to enjoy life. I was visiting an elderly neighbour, Mrs Stacey, recently. She was sitting in a big old-fashioned armchair as we chatted. She told me that the previous day she had been out doing her garden and that although she couldn't do much, what she could do she really enjoyed. She told me that she knew her guardian angel was there, giving her a helping hand. As she talked about the joy she had got out of her gardening two angels appeared, sitting on either side of her. It was as if they were sitting on the arms of the chair. The angels looked like spring. One of them had a simple white daisy in its hands and the other one seemed to have flowers of different sorts and different colours scattered in its lap. These all seemed to be bigger and more abundant versions of flowers that we know – among them were pansies

and more daisies. It was spring and I knew Mrs Stacey's garden wasn't yet in bloom, but I knew that in summer it would be. The angels were there, helping her to learn to enjoy life to the full. We sat there as she told me that she enjoys life so much more now – that she does her best to get pleasure out of all the simple things she might have ignored or taken for granted in the past. She told me how much less important material things seemed to her now. She did admit, though, that she loved both her big armchair and her garden. She told me that when I left she would go for a walk – a short walk as that is all her body would allow now – but that she would enjoy it and she would stop and talk to anyone who crossed her path during the course of the walk.

17

When we allow ourselves to love life we get energised
mentally and physically, and start to see more purpose
in our lives. We become happier and healthier people,
more able to cope with whatever life throws at us.

*The Angel of Hope is a beacon of light in all
our lives. He helps to keep the light of hope burning
inside all of us throughout our lives. Hope plays an
enormous part in everyone's life. Hope makes the
impossible possible. Then we allow ourselves to love
life we get energised mentally and physically, and
start to see more purpose in our lives. We become
happier and healthier people, more able to cope with
whatever life throws at us.*

When you approach work or any task with love-of-life, the task becomes so much easier, you gain more confidence, and start to see the positives in the work you are doing. You realise how much you enjoy your colleagues, or how nice so many of the customers are. When you approach work with this love-of-life you have more mental and physical energy and are able to do a better job. You are open to see and seize opportunities to learn new things, or take on a new job. It helps to move you forward in life.

Lots of people feel called to take on a cause that other people might regard as a burden. Very often their commitment to this cause feeds their love of life and this in turn energises and empowers them to overcome hurdles and barriers that might be put in their way.

The angels have always told me that everyone must continually remind themselves to see the bright points in their everyday life, however small they might seem. Choose to enjoy the little things, to appreciate the cup of tea you are drinking, the flowers in the garden and a smile on a child's face. When someone is down they get out of the habit of appreciating these things, so you need to constantly remind yourself to enjoy the moment, whatever you are doing.

Angels sometimes ask us to help them. Suddenly you feel you should ring someone or walking through the park you suddenly feel you should smile at a stranger or engage them in conversation. It may seem a small or a rather silly thing to us, but it may be that for this person, it is a sign of hope, a message from their angel. As trivial as it may seem to you, it may be very important to them. Children, of course, are naturals at this. Angels communicate much more easily with children and a child will have no hesitation in going up to a complete stranger and saying something, or picking a flower and giving it to them.

As adults, we have to be aware that when a thought comes into our head to do something for someone, even a stranger, we need to just go and do it. We are the angels' messengers and at times it can be hard for the angels to deliver messages or give signs, as so often we are reluctant to pass them on. Sometimes, the sign you are asked to give could save someone's life. They may be very down and desperate, and you are asked to do a little thing, but what may seem a little thing to you could mean so much to someone else.

Never feel that you are not deserving of help. We are all deserving of help and the angels love to help us.

The potential for love is limitless; we are all capable of giving and receiving unlimited love. Loving one person does not mean you have less to give to another. No one is unlovable or undeserving of love, regardless of how you might judge their past actions, and no one is incapable of love.

Prayer is such a powerful force. We underestimate it so much. Prayer can move mountains if only we would let it. If only you realise just how powerful prayer can be, you will never feel hopeless.

No one ever prays alone. When you pray to God there are a multitude of angels of prayer there, praying with you, regardless of your religious faith or how you are behaving. They are there enhancing your prayer, interceding on your behalf.

Summertime

Your guardian angel wants you to know the love that is inside of you. Your guardian angel wants to remind you during these summer months that you are pure love.

Your guardian angel wants to help you to allow yourself to live as freely as the sun shines brightly. Allow the sun to shine on you. See the light of the spiritual side of you just as you see the sun shining in the sky.

Allow that light to come forward and see the abundance of that which is around you: flowers in bloom, fruit upon the trees and the birds in the air. Let yourself go and enjoy all the good things that you recognise in your life. They will be all sizes, big and small, but don't forget to recognise the things that are free this summer: the simple, everyday things.

Do your best to listen to your guardian angel so you can enjoy all the beautiful aspects of summertime.

Love is the most powerful force in the world; it comes from our soul. It's love that brings all the joy and happiness into our lives; it's love that helps to steer us in the right direction and drives us forward, regardless of what is going on in our lives; it's love that makes living worthwhile.

We are all pure love. But most of us have locked away this love within ourselves and don't let it out. This love remains there, though. We can lock love away but we cannot destroy it, and we always have the potential to release it. We release it by learning to love ourselves again first. If we are unable to love ourselves, we are unable to love another.

*One of the most important things we all have to
learn is how to love ourselves more. Instead of seeing
all the imperfections within yourself you need to see
the beauty within yourself. You need to learn to see
yourself as your guardian angel sees you. You need to
allow yourself to see the sweetness, the compassion, the
love that is within you.*

Each and every one of us has a unique role to play in this world. No one else can play your part.

I've been given a prayer by the angels to help you to
release your love:
Dear God, please help me to release that most precious
gift you have given me of love,
That gift of love that comes from Heaven and is
connected to my soul. Amen.

The greater part of our lives is made up of all the small things – the ordinary and the everyday. If we ignore these things or dismiss them as trivial and unimportant we will miss out on life. We will miss out on what is really important. Whether we realise it or not, the big things are made up of a lot of little things.

Whatever happens to us in life we need to keep the door open to new friendships; we need to keep open the possibility that an acquaintance, perhaps one you have hardly noticed, has the potential to become a good friend; that a stranger who you have yet to meet could become a very important friend to you.

Each and every one of our destinies is to live life to the full. This means living every minute of every day to the full and trying to be aware and conscious of every moment and, where possible, to enjoy them all. Your life is today. It's not yesterday or tomorrow. It's now. This moment.

Often, the key to letting love conquer hate is in having the courage to take the first step.

There is always beauty around us. We just don't always notice it and we frequently don't think it is important. It's the little bits of beauty around us that help to teach us to appreciate life.

Many of us think too much about ourselves and about what is best for **me**. *We must think of others and take nothing for granted. Our quality of life improves as we help others because in helping others, we are helping ourselves to feel fulfilled. The self-worth that helping people creates makes us feel more alive.*

Remember strangers give you messages from your angels. Sometimes, someone – it could be a shop assistant, a bus driver, a neighbour's child – says something to you, and you react deeply. It might feel like a sign of encouragement or hope, or like something that someone you love, who is not around, would have said. Listen. Don't doubt your feelings. Don't dismiss these precious moments and fail to acknowledge them.

Angels are great believers in humour. Angels often try and make me laugh, and I see them doing this around people who are out of sorts. Look for opportunities for laughter. Seeing the humour in things can lighten your mood considerably. Even allowing yourself to laugh at a funny movie can be a tonic.

*No matter what is going on in your life, no matter
how tough you may find things, you are here to live
life to the full. The more fully we live life, the more the
angels can help us and guide us through all our ups and
downs. Start to recognise all the wonderful things that
are around you: go out for a walk, and see the beauties
of nature, smile at your neighbours as you pass by.
Most of us take so much for granted. It is only when we
lose something that we realise how precious it really was.*

Recently, we were in the very, busy parking area of a
shopping centre – my daughter Ruth was driving. As we
drove in, the angels whispered in my ear and told me to
look into the car park. I saw an elderly lady who looked
very stressed. Her car was jammed in a corner, with a
big truck parked beside her and another car parked very
closely behind her. I watched as she got in and out of
the car. She walked around her car looking extremely
distressed; she clearly had no idea how she was going to
get it out without damaging something. She was looking
around to see if there was anyone who would help her.
The light of her guardian angel opened up, and spoke

to me without words saying 'Lorna help her. No one is listening'. I noticed lots of angels in the car park whispering in people's ears, I know they noticed her but none of them were prepared to listen to their angel and go and help her. I turned to Ruth and told her that I was going to help the woman. I got out and walked over to the elderly lady. I asked could I help. She was a little hesitant at first. Her guardian angel wrapped himself around her and she started to thaw and relax. She handed me the keys. Her car was very old and she told me it was difficult to get it into reverse. I told her not to worry. I would manage. I sounded confident but I was worried.

Lorna Byrne

The car was stuck in a very tight space and I'm not the greatest parker at the best of times. As I got into the car there was an angel sitting in the passenger seat beside me. I spoke to the angel without words saying, I'm definitely going to need help doing this, there is hardly any room to move the car. The angel told me to look in the mirror. I did. There were lots of angels surrounding the car. 'Just move inch by inch' the angel told me. I did as the angel said, and with the elderly lady standing behind the car guiding me, I reversed out of the tight space. The angel sitting in the passenger seat, told me to tell the elderly lady to move to one side as she was in the way. I did

*and I continued until I had the car out in the open space
where the woman could drive away without any problem.
As I opened the car door to get out I saw that there were
various people including my daughter and an abundance
of angels watching my manoeuvre. The elderly lady gave
me a big hug as she thanked me. She told me she would
pray for me and I told her I would pray for her as well.
Her guardian angel gave me a big smile of gratitude.
We all need to be more pro-active in offering to help
others, showing that we care and having compassion
for each other.*

Autumn

Your guardian angel wants you to consider your life during
this season.

Autumn is also a season when we are shown the magnificent
environment we live our lives in. As you recognise the richness
around you that comes from nature your guardian angel wants
you also to look at yourself and your life to see what you have
accomplished.

As a recognition of the qualities of autumn in your own life,
and as you walk through the third season of the year, say to yourself,
"Yes, I have done brilliantly. I have gotten this far and I know
I can do it!" Look at all you have achieved. Look at all that has
transpired in your life, especially the growth of your spirituality.
Acknowledge the accomplishment of recognising the spiritual
side of yourself.

Look at yourself in the mirror, think of your life, and see the
colours of autumn shining through you.

*In forgiving yourself you give yourself peace and allow
yourself to become more loving to everyone around you.
In forgiving yourself, you forgive everyone around you.
A Prayer for Forgiveness and Peace of Mind*

*God, please forgive me for all my imperfections, for all
the wrong I have done. Give me the grace to forgive those
that have hurt me. Amen.*

We have been given this planet to live in, love and enjoy for our lifetime, but we have also been given the sacred task of passing it on to future generations.

The light of a soul is perfect and crystal clear; no light in the world can resemble the light of a soul in any way, not even the light of the biggest, brightest diamond, because the soul is lit up by the light of God.

If everyone could see the beauty of the human soul, as I do, then there would be no hate or killing or war. When I see the soul of another person, I am overwhelmed by love. This love can conquer hate if only we would let it.

The most important things in our lives are our relationships – from those simple ones with people we pass once in our lives and smile at on a street, to our more in-depth relationships with our families, friends and loved ones. Relationships are priceless. They are much more important than material things, and far too often we take them for granted.

At times we are so busy that we forget to live life and enjoy the ordinary everyday pleasures. We try to cram so much into our busy lives that we actually forget what is important.

Ask your guardian angel to help you enjoy the everyday things more – the simple things of life. Try and practise enjoying and seeing the beauty in the things that are around you. Practise doing it for a few minutes at a time until you get into the habit of it.

We all have to show our vulnerabilities. We all have to learn that it is OK to be vulnerable and that no one is perfect. Friendships are often the best place to show this vulnerability. The next time you are with your friends, observe who is allowing their true selves to show, warts and all, and who is keeping the barriers up, presenting themselves and their lives as perfect. It may be you. If it's others who are not trusting, try to give them the support and encouragement to share more openly.

The angels have told me that deep friendship brings huge responsibility with it. What binds people together in powerful and close friendship is trust, the confidence that you can trust that good friend with everything in your life.

Thinking loving thoughts about friends,
particularly after a rift, is important. In fact, thinking
loving thoughts about anyone and everyone is important.
When we think loving thoughts, we release some more of
the love that we have locked away.

The value of friendship

Friendship helps us to grow and become more caring and understanding. I watched this at work with the supervisor of a supermarket where I have shopped over the years. One day some years ago I was doing my shopping and I saw him surrounded by angels. The angels with him told me that he was being driven crazy by a new young man who had come to work in the store. He was able to deal with it, though, because of what friendship had taught him over the years. The angels told me that over ten years before, when he had started work in the shop, he had considered himself superior to the people who were working for him. He didn't think that work was any place for friendship, and he didn't think any of the people working for him had anything to offer him as a friend.

He certainly wasn't a friend to anyone who worked there, and was a rather cold and uncaring supervisor. One day, though, about six months into the job, he himself made a big mistake on a delivery and was in a state about it. He feared he would lose his job. One of the people who worked for him came and told him not to worry, that he and some of the other colleagues would help to sort the problem out. They did. The angels told me that this was the first time that he had lowered his barriers to allow friendship into his place of work. His friendships over the years at work had given him an insight into lots of different people. This man had learnt a lot and this is what gave him the patience to work with the new young colleague, even if he was irritating him.

One thing God and the angels have always said to me is that they only ask us to do the best we can. They aren't asking for more than that, but we must try.

We are all responsible for trying to ensure that as little love as possible is locked away within children. Children are our future, and the only way for the world to evolve as I have been shown it should be is for each generation to be more loving and compassionate than the one before. This is only possible if we support the children around us, and protect and encourage them so that they don't need to lock their love away.

We all need to be aware when tough things happen

to us, that we have a choice of how to respond.

Responding with anger and hate may be an automatic

response, but it is never the best one. When we respond

with hate we shut away more of our own love. Be

aware when your first thought is to respond with hate,

you do have a choice.

As we become more spiritually aware we become more compassionate, more given to seeing the good in others, and this makes us gentler and kinder.

Winter

Your guardian angel wants you to look upon your hopes and dreams. Be thoughtful and see all the things that are possible in your life. Winter is a time to recognise all the things that have inspired you during the year.

As you enter winter the trees have gone to sleep. Many animals and insects hibernate The year is coming to an end, and you are at the end of a journey – an incredible journey.

Smile at all the things you treasure now: the love in your life, new friends, your spiritual growth, your work, a new home, that puppy even.

The days are getting shorter, so you are finding time to reflect, to be silent within yourself, and to know who you are. You can recognise the love and joy in your heart. You can feel how your spiritual journey of being closer to your guardian angel has opened your heart.

Take that chance winter provides to dwell on all the love that you have inside of you and all the love you have allowed into your life to be shared with others.

Winter is a time of celebrations. Give thanks for the happiness and fulfilment you have found in life.

You are resting now in winter and looking forward to springtime again, the time of new beginnings. Your guardian angel has been there with you all the time and you have listened. Well done.

We can be a light, however briefly, in someone else's life.

No one is unloved. If you feel that no loves and cares for you – you are wrong. Your guardian angel is there behind every moment of your life, and is pouring its love out on you continually.

I see a lot of angels holding lights in front of people, helping to encourage them. When I see an angel holding a light in front of someone, I know that the person is having a tough time and that the angel is holding the light to help to give them hope and the courage to keep on going.

Ask your guardian angel to allow you to feel its love –
even a little of it. You can ask by talking to your guardian
angel silently or aloud. I talk to my guardian angel as
I do to my friends.

Nobody dies alone. There is no need to have a fear of dying. When that last moment comes, it is free of pain and you go willingly. You are not on your own. Your guardian angel is there with you, as are a lot of other angels. People you love who have died before you are there too, to welcome you and reassure you that there is no need to have any fear. Some people may have pain right up until that last moment, but at that last moment there is none. Death is like birth. I know you might think that's weird, but you are being born into a new life. You actually don't 'die', it's only this body or shell that you leave, like an egg shell. You are much more than just a body. You are body and soul and your soul never dies.

Long before I started to write, a woman called Maura –
who used to come and see me – told me a lovely story
of how the angels had comforted her one Christmas after
her husband had died. Christmas can be a sad time for
people who have lost someone they love. This Christmas,
Maura was at her kitchen sink, washing dishes and
remembering the good times when her husband and her
children were all together – the birthdays, christenings,
but particularly the Christmases. Her children were all
grown up now, but were still very close to her. She had
a wonderful family but that didn't fill the loneliness of
missing the man she had loved dearly. She was feeling so
sad and so alone and there were tears in her eyes as she
begged, 'Just give me a sign.

*Show me that you really are there, that you haven't
gone away completely'. She followed some instinct and
just left the dishes in the sink and walked across the
kitchen and out into the garden. The weather was cold
and changeable and she stood there in the cold looking
around her, wondering to herself whether her husband
could really be in Heaven, whether he could still be with
her in spirit. She looked at trees and plants that had
grown since he had died and then, out of nowhere it
seemed to her, it started to snow. Maura laughed and,
feeling her husband's presence in some way, she spoke
to him aloud. 'So you have me out in the garden, and now
it's starting to snow, I'm freezing and it's snowing.'
The snowflakes kept falling and then, for no reason she*

could explain, one falling snowflake attracted her. It was no different from any of the other snowflakes that were falling around her but she had a very strong urge to catch that particular snowflake. She reached out and the snowflake landed on her hand. She looked at it in amazement. The snowflake wasn't melting. As she looked more closely she realised that it wasn't a snowflake. It was a feather, a tiny feather no bigger than a snowflake. There were no birds around. There was nowhere it could have come from. As she touched the feather, tears came into her eyes and she said a heartfelt thank-you. She thanked God and the angels and she thanked her much-loved husband. Receiving this little feather filled Maura's heart with joy.

She knew it was a sign that her husband was happy in Heaven, but that he was still with her whenever she needed him. It gave her the hope and strength to face the future, to know that she wasn't alone. Maura always had faith, but this feather rekindled her faith and her belief that her husband's soul was in Heaven. That she would see him again one day. She held that little feather tightly in her hand as she walked back into the house to look for something small and special to put her precious feather in, so that she could keep it safe and look at it, and know that her husband was there with her in spirit and that God and His angels were there with her also.

I see angels surrounding and comforting people who are feeling grief. But, often, we are so grief stricken and desolate that we don't feel this consolation. Try and remind yourself that these angels are there with you. Angels will give us signs of encouragement, particularly at this time, and often they work through others who come to console us or to offer words of support.

A Prayer for Hard Times

God, Pour the grace of hope upon me and allow me always to see the light of hope burning brightly in front of me. Light up the darkness by filling me with faith and hope and allowing me to receive the comfort of your love. Give me the courage and strength to know that I will get through these hard times. Fill me with the joy and trust of knowing that I am your child and that you will care for me and those I love. Hear my prayer. Amen.

There is so much more to life than material objects. Often we think these are the only important things, but in doing so, we miss so much else.

It's important that we reach out and try and help someone when that person has had a disappointment, a row, or feels down in some way. We are all connected, so it's important that we take responsibility for others who cross our paths, not just close friends or relatives.

Every one of us has the grace of healing within us.
Whenever you feel moved to help someone who is hurting
– someone you love or someone you have never even met –
you are using the grace of healing. Love and compassion
release the healing power that is within you.

A Christmas Prayer of Hope

My God, I ask you this Christmas for the gift of the Angel of Hope to come into my life, into the lives of those I love, and into the lives of everyone in the world in need of hope at this time. Amen.

Take the time to enjoy this Christmas. In today's world we rush around a lot, but the angels tell me that in doing so, we often forget what life is really about. Life is not just about work, hurrying and deadlines. We need to stop for a moment and see the beauty in people around us and allow the goodness of people to penetrate our lives. We need time to sit down and have relaxed conversation with family and friends, with people who we may not know well and sometimes with complete strangers. We need to take the time to realize how lucky we are to be alive.

The period from November until January is not just a
time of celebration in many religions, it is also a time
of the intertwining of the old and the new years and is
a time of new beginnings across many cultures. We have
the potential for new beginnings all year round, but most
of us are inclined to ignore this potential because we are
afraid of change. Or we simply don't even make the time
to imagine what change for the better would look like
in our lives. We have so many potential destinies, but we
grasp so few. We forget that each and every day we have
the potential for new starts in our lives.

*New beginnings don't have to be big and dramatic.
They are not usually about winning the lottery, moving
country or becoming famous. New beginnings are often
about having a change of attitude about ourselves. So
many of us lock away our true selves because of hurt or
pain or because we feel inadequate. Allow yourself to feel
love and compassion for yourself. If you could only see
what the angels show me about how unnecessarily hard
we make our lives, you would have to smile. The most
powerful new beginning anyone can make is to allow love
– love for yourself and love for others – to grow.*

Remember, we are the guardian angels of nature.
Enjoy the beauty that is around you. The angels
are always trying to get you to notice the beauty
of the world.

**Prayer of Thy Healing Angels that is carried
from God by Micheal Thy Archangel.**

Pour out Thy Healing Angels,
Thy Heavenly Host upon me
and upon those that I love.
Let me feel the beam of Thy Healing Angels
upon me, the light of Your Healing Hand.
I will let Thy Healing begin
Whatever way God grants it. Amen.

Picture Credits